FOUND ALL AROUND

A Show-and-Tell of Found Poetry

Written by Krishna Dalal
Illustrated by Karen Heathwood

ONE WORD
PUBLISHING

Published by One Word Publishing
1103 Shelter Bay Avenue, Mill Valley, CA 94941
www.onewordpublishing.com

Publisher's Cataloging-In-Publication Data
(Prepared by The Donohue Group, Inc.)

Dalal, Krishna.
  Found all around : a show-and-tell of found poetry / written by Krishna Dalal ; illustrated by Karen Heathwood.

   pages : color illustrations ; cm

   Summary: A how-to poetry book that not only includes found poems, but also illustrates the origin and process of each poem. Found poetry is a form of poetry where words are taken from existing text (newspapers, menus, books, etc.), reordered, and turned into a poem.
  Interest age level: 006-010.
  ISBN: 978-0-9833245-2-2

  1. Children's poetry, American. 2. Poetry--Authorship--Juvenile literature. 3. Children's poetry, American. 4. Poetry--Authorship. I. Heathwood, Karen. II. Title.

PS36204.A535 F68 2014
811/.6   2014913255

Printed in the United States of America

For two brothers who have always been there for me - Nrupesh and Chirag.

- K.D.

To my Mum who taught me that art, like poetry, IS all around.

- K.H.

What is Found Poetry?

Step 1

Select interesting words from any text.

Reading poetry can be moving, thought-provoking, and beautiful. Writing poetry, however, can cause anxiety and dread. The goal of this book is to dispel that fear. With just a little imagination and creativity, anyone can write a great poem. One form of poetry that makes it easier than ever before is found poetry.

In found poetry, you take words from existing text (newspapers, menus, books, street signs, etc.), reorder them, and turn them into a poem. Writing this form of poetry is like a treasure hunt. You look for interesting words, put them together in different ways, and see what comes out – it's the literary form of a collage!

This book is not just a collection of poems; it is a guide on writing found poetry. Whether you simply look through this book, or buy it, the poems will fill you with glee and the process will inspire you. Soon, you'll know how to easily create your own found poems. You will be a poet!

Step 2

Rearrange words.

poetry writing dread this fear it before

you take turn into look book buy poet

glee you'll know a be a

Step 3

Create a Poem!

dread writing poetry

turn fear into glee

take a look

buy this book

before you know it

you'll be a great poet

He **FOUND**

a poem

in a newspaper.

Today in Sports History — The first rules of baseball were written in 1845 for the Knickerbockers Base Ball Club.

July 1, 2014

Dunn Does It Again

By Allison Kegley

Stepping onto the baseball field, Mike Dunn forgets the ups and downs of previous games. "You should play in the moment. I don't think about where, or how, I played last week," explains Dunn.

That might be easy for Dunn to say, who is in a class of his own this season. After swatting three home runs against the Tigers Sunday night, Dunn now leads all hitters in AVG (.387) while placing second in OBP (.453) and SLG (.634). He also has the highest OPS (1.116) and most RBIs (127). In terms of the math, he earns the title of 'Best Hitter'.

Nevertheless, Dunn understands that a higher batting average doesn't necessarily translate to a better win-loss ratio for his team. "I know it's vital that

Mike Dunn hits one to the bleachers.

we also focus on our fielding percentage," says Dunn. "Lynn's improved his pitching velocity, and we've decreased our errors. We need to approach the game from a different angle. We need to go the distance."

Saturday's Local Events
High School Girls Soccer:
BHS Tournament, 2 p.m.

SAN FRANCISCO (N)	ab	r	h	bl
Enochs, rf	3	0	0	0
Bulloch, 2b	4	0	1	1
Jack, cf	3	2	0	1
Maddie, lf	4	1	0	0
Dalzell, c	2	0	0	0
Total	16	3	1	2

CHICAGO (N)	ab	r	h	bl
Slusser, rf	3	0	0	0
Carrillo, 2b	2	0	1	0
Sully, cf	3	2	0	1
Duan, lf	1	4	0	0
Luke, c	4	0	0	0
Total	13	6	1	1

She **FOUND**

a po•em

in a dic•tion•ar•y

dance *–v.* **danced, danc·ing, danc·es 1** to tremble, move back and forth **2** To move the body and feet in rhythm, ordinarily to music **3** to move lightly and gaily; caper **4** to bob up and down **5** to be stirred into rapid movement, as leaves in a wind **6** to slide, or to move in a graceful way *–n.* **1** rhythmic movement of the body and feet, ordinarily to music **2** a particular kind of dance, as the waltz, tango, etc. **3** the art of dancing, esp. as performed in ballet or modern dance SYN. move, flutter, glide, prance, perform

dandelion *n.* **dan·de·li·on** any of several plants (genus *Taraxacum*) of the composite family, common weeds with jagged leaves, often used as greens, and yellow flowers

genus Taraxacum

Dance of the Dandelion

(music performed by the wind)

back and forth
up and down
flutter of a ballet
glide of a waltz
tremble of a tango

a common weed,
stirred into a graceful flower

They **FOUND**
a poem
in a menu.

The Fussy Herbivore
restaurant

THE FUSSY HERBIVORE
Dinner Menu

Sautéed Green Beans	7
with tomatoes and basil	
Grilled Asparagus	7
with lemon garlic butter	
Steamed Artichokes	8
with herb-caper mayonnaise	
Pan-fried Kale	9
with walnuts	
Roasted Cauliflower	11
with Béchamel cheese sauce	
Boiled Potatoes	12
with mushroom ketchup	

Thank you for dining with us.
We select only the freshest, local ingredients.
All plants were treated humanely and died mercifully.
Yes, substitutions are honored – we make it your way.
Prices listed without tax.
Gratuity not included, unless party of 10 or more.
No smoking, please.

2031 Dodia Lane | Happy Valley | 555 1234

Poem Ingredients

fuss
sauteed
grilled
asparagus
steamed
with
fried
roasted
cheese
boiled
ketchup

for
us
we
and
died
yes
way
without
not
unless
no
please

Aspara-gross

Asparagus?
    Not for us.
    Not without fuss.

Grilled?
Roasted?
Sautéed?
    No way!

Steamed?
Boiled?
Fried?
    Not unless we died!

With ketchup and cheese?
Yes, please!

He **FOUND**
a poem
from street signs.

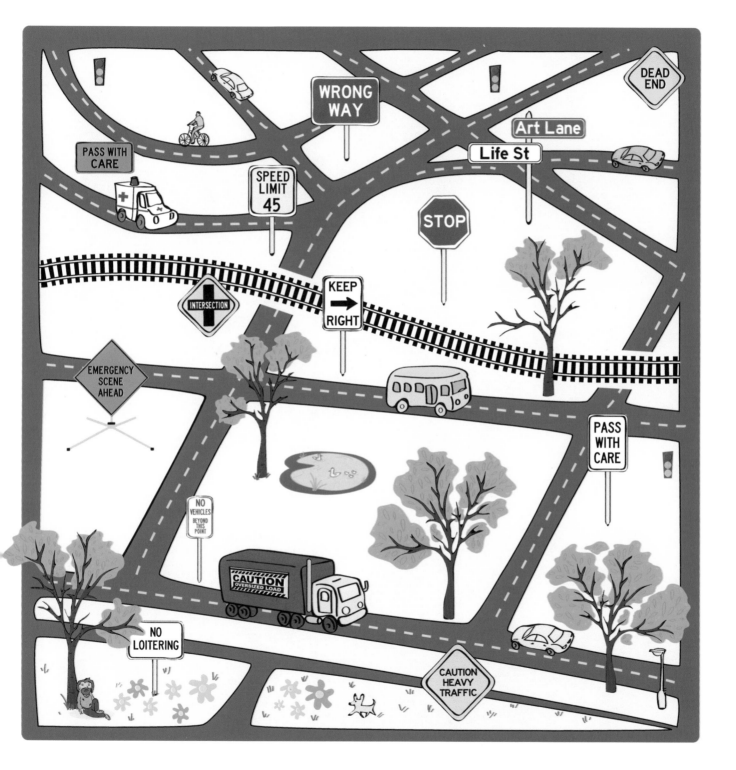

Mulling over Murals

Stop,
Loiter,
Oversized art this way

Caution: heavy scenes ahead
At the intersection of right and wrong,
Life and death

Art with no limits
Art with a point

Stop,
Loiter

She **FOUND**
a poem
in a flier.

BEWARE
Wild Animal Sightings

Beware: mountain lions, bears, and wolves have been spotted in this area.

General Information

These wild animals are not out for destruction and typically avoid human contact. However, precautions should always be taken. Walk in groups and make lots of noise. Keep children with you at all times. Sounds these wild beasts might make include growls, rumbles, or barks. These sounds do not always signal aggression.

Never feed wild animals.
They have a keen sense of smell, and sharp claws and teeth. If they associate hunger and food with humans, they will become more aggressive in seeking food outside of their natural habitat.

Wild Animal Encounter

If you encounter one of these wild animals, stop. Don't run. Speak in a calm, assertive voice. Face the animal, but avoid direct eye contact. Pick up small children so they do not panic and run. Make yourself big and back away slowly.

He **FOUND** a poem in an orchestra.

ROYAL ROAR ORCHESTRA

Jonathan Caulfield, Conductor

Sunday Evening, January 3, 2014, at 8:30
HILL AUDITORIUM

PROGRAM (PART I)

Canon In D... Pachelbel
Peer Gynt: In The Hall Of The Mountain King .... Grieg
Midsummer Night's Dream: Wedding March .... Mendelssohn
Tale Of Tsar Saltan: Flight Of The Bumblebee .... Rimsky-Korsakov
Moonlight Sonata .... Beethoven
Nutcracker: Dance Of The Sugar-Plum Fairy .... Tchaikovsky

PROGRAM (PART II)

Entry Of The Gladiators .... Fucik
Nutcracker: Waltz Of The Flowers .... Tchaikovsky
Four Seasons: Spring .... Vivaldi
Light Cavalry Overture .... Suppé
Four Seasons: Winter .... Vivaldi
The Planets: Mars, The Bringer Of War .... Holst

Instruments of the Orchestra
Strings: first violins, second violins, violas, cellos, double basses
Woodwinds: flutes, oboes, clarinets, bassoons
Brass: trumpets, trombones, tubas, french horns
Percussion: timpani, snare drums, bass drums, cymbals

Ode to Our Senses

(Flute) fairy's flight in the moonlight
(Trumpet) king's entry with his cavalry
(Drums) canon's roar through a winter war
(Violin) bumblebee's dream of flowers in spring

She **FOUND**
a poem
in her homework
and her diary.

Dear Diary,

Siblings are the worst! Their only purpose is to make me miserable! My older brother is so bossy and such a big bully. He has quite the temper and is always ready for a fight. He also thinks he's the best – so special, and always right. But my younger sister is even worse! She's such a little crybaby and always wants to hang out with me. When my friends come over, she tells mom and dad that we don't play with her and exclude her from our club. Then dad says I need to apologize at once and be more polite. Boy, what a pest!

This DIARY belongs to
Avni

Avni Shah
September 30, 2014

(A-)

Our solar system has eight planets. Mercury is the closest one to the sun. Its (sp.) also the smallest. The next planet is Venus. It's so bright and burns much hotter than all the rest of the planets. Earth is the third planet from the sun. It has water and life. Mars is nicknamed the "Red Planet", and Jupiter is the largest. Jupiter is larger than all of the other planets put together! Saturn has many beautiful rings and is the sixth planet from the sun. Uranus is tilted on its side. Neptune is the farthest from the sun. It's (sp.) surface is a beautiful blue color. Pluto used to be a planet, but now it's not. They call it a dwarf planet.

who is 'They'?

Planets Make the Worst Siblings
(as told by Pluto)

Jupiter the largest
A big bully to the rest
Earth with water and life
Thinks it's the best
Uranus tilted on its side
Boy, what a pest

Mars the "Red Planet"
Always ready for a fight
Neptune a beautiful blue
Not once polite
Venus burns so hot and bright
Quite the temper all right

Saturn with its many rings
Beautiful but bossy
Mercury the smallest one
Such a crybaby
Excluded from their special club
"Dwarf" they all call me

They **FOUND**
a poem
at the library.

Charlie and the Chocolate Factory (Roald Dahl)

How to Train Your Dragon (Cressida Cowell)

The Mouse and the Motorcycle (Beverly Cleary)

The Lion, the Witch and the Wardrobe (C.S. Lewis)

The Wonderful Wizard of Oz (L. Frank Baum)

The Upstairs Room (Johanna Reiss)

The Castle in the Attic (Elizabeth Winthrop)

Holes (Louis Sachar)

Magic Tree House (Mary Pope Osborne)

The Wind in the Willows (Kenneth Grahame)

Blood on the River (Elisa Carbone)

Walk Two Moons (Sharon Creech)

By the Great Horn Spoon! (Sid Fleischman)

The Ordinary Princess (M. M. Kaye)

I am the Cheese (Robert Cormier)

Riding Freedom (Pam Muñoz Ryan)

Roll of Thunder, Hear My Cry (Mildred D. Taylor)

The Family Under the Bridge (Natalie Savage Carlson)

Say no to summer boredom and earn an armload of great prizes by joining our summer reading program. All you will need to do is register at the front desk.

- Ms. LaMond & Ms. Klein (Librarians)

County Library

SUMMER READING List

Imagine That!

A castle in a mouse hole
A cheese factory on the moon

A wizard under a willow tree
A chocolate river in my room

A princess walking a dragon
A witch riding a spoon

How? Magic?
No, an ordinary # 2 will do.

CPSIA information can be obtained at www.ICGtesting.com
Printed in the USA
BVIW12n0949010517
482556BV00024B/232

9 780983 324522